WORD OF LIFE

SERMON NOTEBOOK FOR MEN

BY
WORD SPAN PUBLISHING, INC.

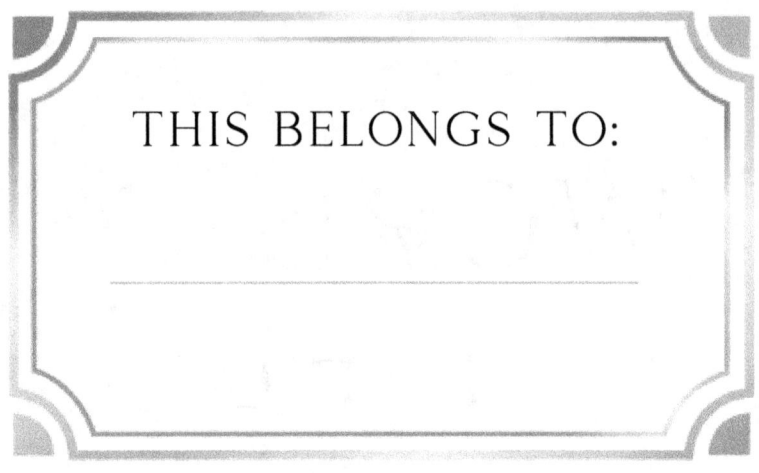

THIS BELONGS TO:

_____

Word of Life:
Sermon Notebook for Men

ISBN: 978-1-961095-01-4

THE
WORD OF LIFE

"In the beginning was the Word, and the Word was with God, and the Word was God. In Him was life, and that life was the light of men."

John 1: 1&4

*The Holy Bible, New International Version

Date:

Speaker:

Topic:

Scripture References:

Notes:

_____

_____

_____

_____

_____

_____

_____

_____

_____

_____

_____

_____

Key Points:

_____

_____

_____

_____

_____

_____

_____

Thoughts & Reflections:

Prayer Request:

Date:

Speaker:

Topic:

Scripture References:

Notes:

_____

_____

_____

_____

_____

_____

_____

_____

_____

_____

Key Points:

_____

_____

_____

_____

_____

_____

_____

Thoughts & Reflections:

Prayer Request:

Date:

Speaker:

Topic:

Scripture References:

Notes:

_____

_____

_____

_____

_____

_____

_____

_____

_____

_____

_____

Key Points:

_____

_____

_____

_____

_____

_____

_____

Thoughts & Reflections:

Prayer Request:

Date:	Speaker:

Topic:

Scripture References:

Notes:

_____

_____

_____

_____

_____

_____

_____

_____

_____

_____

Key Points:

_____

_____

_____

_____

_____

_____

_____

Thoughts & Reflections:

Prayer Request:

Date:

Speaker:

Topic:

Scripture References:

Notes:

_____

_____

_____

_____

_____

_____

_____

_____

_____

_____

_____

_____

_____

Key Points:

_____

_____

_____

_____

_____

_____

_____

Thoughts & Reflections:

Prayer Request:

Date:

Speaker:

Topic:

Scripture References:

Notes:

_____

_____

_____

_____

_____

_____

_____

_____

_____

_____

_____

_____

Key Points:

_____

_____

_____

_____

_____

_____

_____

Thoughts & Reflections:

Prayer Request:

Date:

Speaker:

Topic:

Scripture References:

Notes:

_____

_____

_____

_____

_____

_____

_____

_____

_____

_____

_____

_____

Key Points:

_____

_____

_____

_____

_____

_____

_____

Thoughts & Reflections:

Prayer Request:

Date:

Speaker:

Topic:

Scripture References:

Notes:

_____

_____

_____

_____

_____

_____

_____

_____

_____

_____

_____

_____

Key Points:

_____

_____

_____

_____

_____

_____

_____

Thoughts & Reflections:

Prayer Request:

Date: Speaker:

Topic:

Scripture References:

Notes:

_____

_____

_____

_____

_____

_____

_____

_____

_____

_____

_____

Key Points:

_____

_____

_____

_____

_____

_____

_____

Thoughts & Reflections:

Prayer Request:

Date: Speaker:

Topic:

Scripture References:

Notes:

_____

_____

_____

_____

_____

_____

_____

_____

_____

_____

_____

Key Points:

_____

_____

_____

_____

_____

_____

_____

Thoughts & Reflections:

Prayer Request:

Date:

Speaker:

Topic:

Scripture References:

Notes:

_____

_____

_____

_____

_____

_____

_____

_____

_____

_____

_____

Key Points:

_____

_____

_____

_____

_____

_____

_____

Thoughts & Reflections:

Prayer Request:

Date:

Speaker:

Topic:

Scripture References:

Notes:

_____

_____

_____

_____

_____

_____

_____

_____

_____

_____

_____

Key Points:

_____

_____

_____

_____

_____

_____

_____

Thoughts & Reflections:

Prayer Request:

Date:

Speaker:

Topic:

Scripture References:

Notes:

_____

_____

_____

_____

_____

_____

_____

_____

_____

_____

_____

Key Points:

_____

_____

_____

_____

_____

_____

_____

Thoughts & Reflections:

Prayer Request:

Date:

Speaker:

Topic:

Scripture References:

Notes:

_____

_____

_____

_____

_____

_____

_____

_____

_____

_____

_____

_____

Key Points:

_____

_____

_____

_____

_____

_____

_____

_____

Thoughts & Reflections:

Prayer Request:

Date:

Speaker:

Topic:

Scripture References:

Notes:
_____
_____
_____
_____
_____
_____
_____
_____
_____
_____
_____

Key Points:

_____

_____

_____

_____

_____

_____

_____

_____

Thoughts & Reflections:

Prayer Request:

Date:

Speaker:

Topic:

Scripture References:

Notes:

_____

_____

_____

_____

_____

_____

_____

_____

_____

_____

_____

_____

Key Points:

_____

_____

_____

_____

_____

_____

_____

Thoughts & Reflections:

Prayer Request:

Date:

Speaker:

Topic:

Scripture References:

Notes:

_____

_____

_____

_____

_____

_____

_____

_____

_____

_____

_____

_____

Key Points:

_____

_____

_____

_____

_____

_____

_____

Thoughts & Reflections:

Prayer Request:

Date:

Speaker:

Topic:

Scripture References:

Notes:

_____

_____

_____

_____

_____

_____

_____

_____

_____

_____

_____

_____

Key Points:

_____

_____

_____

_____

_____

_____

_____

Thoughts & Reflections:

Prayer Request:

Date: | Speaker:

Topic:

Scripture References:

Notes:

_____

_____

_____

_____

_____

_____

_____

_____

_____

_____

Key Points:

_____

_____

_____

_____

_____

_____

_____

_____

Thoughts & Reflections:

Prayer Request:

Date:

Speaker:

Topic:

Scripture References:

Notes:

_____

_____

_____

_____

_____

_____

_____

_____

_____

_____

_____

Key Points:

_____

_____

_____

_____

_____

_____

_____

_____

Thoughts & Reflections:

Prayer Request:

Date:

Speaker:

Topic:

Scripture References:

Notes:

_____

_____

_____

_____

_____

_____

_____

_____

_____

_____

_____

Key Points:

_____

_____

_____

_____

_____

_____

_____

_____

Thoughts & Reflections:

Prayer Request:

Date:

Speaker:

Topic:

Scripture References:

Notes:

_____

_____

_____

_____

_____

_____

_____

_____

_____

_____

_____

Key Points:

_____

_____

_____

_____

_____

_____

_____

Thoughts & Reflections:

Prayer Request:

Date: | Speaker:

Topic:

Scripture References:

Notes:

_____

_____

_____

_____

_____

_____

_____

_____

_____

_____

_____

Key Points:

_____

_____

_____

_____

_____

_____

_____

Thoughts & Reflections:

Prayer Request:

Date:

Speaker:

Topic:

Scripture References:

Notes:

_____

_____

_____

_____

_____

_____

_____

_____

_____

_____

_____

Key Points:

_____

_____

_____

_____

_____

_____

_____

Thoughts & Reflections:

Prayer Request:

Date:

Speaker:

Topic:

Scripture References:

Notes:

_____

_____

_____

_____

_____

_____

_____

_____

_____

_____

_____

Key Points:

_____

_____

_____

_____

_____

_____

_____

Thoughts & Reflections:

Prayer Request:

Date:

Speaker:

Topic:

Scripture References:

Notes:

_____

_____

_____

_____

_____

_____

_____

_____

_____

_____

_____

_____

Key Points:

_____

_____

_____

_____

_____

_____

_____

_____

Thoughts & Reflections:

Prayer Request:

Date: | Speaker:

Topic:

Scripture References:

Notes:

_____

_____

_____

_____

_____

_____

_____

_____

_____

_____

_____

_____

Key Points:

_____

_____

_____

_____

_____

_____

_____

Thoughts & Reflections:

Prayer Request:

Date:

Speaker:

Topic:

Scripture References:

Notes:

Key Points:

_____

_____

_____

_____

_____

_____

_____

Thoughts & Reflections:

Prayer Request:

Date:

Speaker:

Topic:

Scripture References:

Notes:

Key Points:

_____

_____

_____

_____

_____

_____

_____

Thoughts & Reflections:

Prayer Request:

Date:

Speaker:

Topic:

Scripture References:

Notes:

_____

_____

_____

_____

_____

_____

_____

_____

_____

_____

Key Points:

_____

_____

_____

_____

_____

_____

_____

Thoughts & Reflections:

Prayer Request:

Date:

Speaker:

Topic:

Scripture References:

Notes:

_____

_____

_____

_____

_____

_____

_____

_____

_____

_____

_____

Key Points:

_____

_____

_____

_____

_____

_____

_____

Thoughts & Reflections:

Prayer Request:

Date:

Speaker:

Topic:

Scripture References:

Notes:

_____

_____

_____

_____

_____

_____

_____

_____

_____

_____

_____

_____

Key Points:

_____

_____

_____

_____

_____

_____

_____

Thoughts & Reflections:

Prayer Request:

Date: | Speaker:

Topic:

Scripture References:

Notes:

_____

_____

_____

_____

_____

_____

_____

_____

_____

_____

_____

Key Points:

_____

_____

_____

_____

_____

_____

_____

Thoughts & Reflections:

Prayer Request:

Date: | Speaker:

Topic:

Scripture References:

Notes:

_____

_____

_____

_____

_____

_____

_____

_____

_____

_____

_____

Key Points:

_____

_____

_____

_____

_____

_____

_____

Thoughts & Reflections:

Prayer Request:

Date:

Speaker:

Topic:

Scripture References:

Notes:

_____

_____

_____

_____

_____

_____

_____

_____

_____

_____

Key Points:

_____

_____

_____

_____

_____

_____

_____

Thoughts & Reflections:

Prayer Request:

Date:

Speaker:

Topic:

Scripture References:

Notes:
_____

_____

_____

_____

_____

_____

_____

_____

_____

_____

_____

Key Points:

_____

_____

_____

_____

_____

_____

_____

Thoughts & Reflections:

Prayer Request:

Date:

Speaker:

Topic:

Scripture References:

Notes:

_____

_____

_____

_____

_____

_____

_____

_____

_____

_____

_____

Key Points:

_____

_____

_____

_____

_____

_____

_____

Thoughts & Reflections:

Prayer Request:

Date:

Speaker:

Topic:

Scripture References:

Notes:

_____

_____

_____

_____

_____

_____

_____

_____

_____

_____

_____

Key Points:

_____

_____

_____

_____

_____

_____

_____

Thoughts & Reflections:

Prayer Request:

Date:

Speaker:

Topic:

Scripture References:

Notes:

_____

_____

_____

_____

_____

_____

_____

_____

_____

_____

_____

_____

Key Points:

_____

_____

_____

_____

_____

_____

_____

Thoughts & Reflections:

Prayer Request:

Date:

Speaker:

Topic:

Scripture References:

Notes:

_____

_____

_____

_____

_____

_____

_____

_____

_____

_____

Key Points:

_____

_____

_____

_____

_____

_____

_____

Thoughts & Reflections:

Prayer Request:

Date: Speaker:

Topic:

Scripture References:

Notes:

_____

_____

_____

_____

_____

_____

_____

_____

_____

_____

_____

Key Points:

_____

_____

_____

_____

_____

_____

_____

Thoughts & Reflections:

Prayer Request:

Date:

Speaker:

Topic:

Scripture References:

Notes:
_____

_____

_____

_____

_____

_____

_____

_____

_____

_____

_____

_____

Key Points:

_____

_____

_____

_____

_____

_____

_____

Thoughts & Reflections:

Prayer Request:

Date:

Speaker:

Topic:

Scripture References:

Notes:

_____

_____

_____

_____

_____

_____

_____

_____

_____

_____

_____

Key Points:

_____

_____

_____

_____

_____

_____

_____

Thoughts & Reflections:

Prayer Request:

Date:

Speaker:

Topic:

Scripture References:

Notes:

_____

_____

_____

_____

_____

_____

_____

_____

_____

_____

_____

_____

Key Points:

_____

_____

_____

_____

_____

_____

_____

Thoughts & Reflections:

Prayer Request:

Date:

Speaker:

Topic:

Scripture References:

Notes:

_____

_____

_____

_____

_____

_____

_____

_____

_____

_____

_____

_____

Key Points:

_____

_____

_____

_____

_____

_____

_____

Thoughts & Reflections:

Prayer Request:

Date: | Speaker:

Topic:

Scripture References:

Notes:

_____

_____

_____

_____

_____

_____

_____

_____

_____

_____

Key Points:

_____

_____

_____

_____

_____

_____

_____

_____

Thoughts & Reflections:

Prayer Request:

Date:

Speaker:

Topic:

Scripture References:

Notes:

_____

_____

_____

_____

_____

_____

_____

_____

_____

_____

Key Points:

_____

_____

_____

_____

_____

_____

_____

Thoughts & Reflections:

Prayer Request:

Date:

Speaker:

Topic:

Scripture References:

Notes:

_____

_____

_____

_____

_____

_____

_____

_____

_____

_____

_____

Key Points:

_____

_____

_____

_____

_____

_____

_____

Thoughts & Reflections:

Prayer Request:

Date: | Speaker:

Topic:

Scripture References:

Notes:

_____

_____

_____

_____

_____

_____

_____

_____

_____

_____

_____

Key Points:

_____

_____

_____

_____

_____

_____

_____

Thoughts & Reflections:

Prayer Request:

Date:

Speaker:

Topic:

Scripture References:

Notes:

_____

_____

_____

_____

_____

_____

_____

_____

_____

_____

_____

Key Points:

_____

_____

_____

_____

_____

_____

_____

Thoughts & Reflections:

Prayer Request:

Date:

Speaker:

Topic:

Scripture References:

Notes:

_____

_____

_____

_____

_____

_____

_____

_____

_____

_____

_____

Key Points:

_____

_____

_____

_____

_____

_____

_____

Thoughts & Reflections:

Prayer Request:

Date: Speaker:

Topic:

Scripture References:

Notes:

_____

_____

_____

_____

_____

_____

_____

_____

_____

_____

_____

_____

Key Points:

_____

_____

_____

_____

_____

_____

_____

Thoughts & Reflections:

Prayer Request:

GOD BLESS!

Please take a quick moment to review this book and show your support for independent publishers.

Thank You!